If You're Looking for a Victim… Keep Looking!

Dan Skoczylas

In memory of those who were taken from us too soon by senseless, random acts of violence. May they rest in eternal peace.
To those who will inevitably be forced to look evil in the eye someday in the future,
I hope placing the proper value on the gift of life gives you the strength to prevail.

I can do all things through Christ, who strengthens me.

Philippians 4:13

Foreward

I am pleased and honored to write the Foreword to Dan's book. I first met Lieutenant Dan Skoczylas in the 90s. I was a Federal Agent investigating high-level narcotics and money laundering criminals in some of the worst areas of Chicago. Dan was part of a Federal Task Force which included several local police officers from surrounding municipalities. This team was responsible for the disruption and dismantlement of major criminal organizations and seizure of multi-kilo quantities of cocaine that were destined for the streets of Chicago and its neighboring suburbs. The key to the success of the Task Force relied primarily on Dan and other police officers' ability to assess a situation on the street and take appropriate action. I refer to that as "street smarts." Others would categorize it as "situational awareness." In his book, Dan does an amazing job describing active shooter events and real life experiences. Each chapter teaches a lesson and makes you think of how you would react in that particular situation. You can't help but put yourself in that scenario as he walks you through the multiple options in order to survive the ordeal.

Dan has researched human behavior during active shooter incidents and helps us understand how unprepared our mind and bodies are throughout an event. Nonetheless, he stresses the importance of having your own plan and disrupting the shooter's strategy as he tries to predict your actions. The need to prepare yourself and make split second decisions could save your life.

Now retired, I can reflect on my personal experiences and be thankful for all the survival training I received. Many of the skills and techniques Dan talks about in his book are the ones that have helped save me and fellow Agents around the world.

Luis M. Alvarez
Deputy Assistant Secretary (Retired)
U.S. Department of Homeland Security

1

The World is Not Evil,
But There is Evil in the World:

A snapshot of the increasing active shooter threat

The Department of Homeland Security defines an active shooter as "an individual actively engaged in killing or attempting to kill people in a populated area."[1] This definition is indeed important for establishing statistics. But this definition is not beneficial to the very people that it describes; the intended victims in the heat of an active shooter incident.

I was a law enforcement officer for more than twenty-four years in a small suburb near the city of Chicago. I was exceptionally blessed over the course of my career to have a complete menu of opportunities as a police officer. I was a federal task force officer, detective sergeant, and a lieutenant. I worked everything from patrol to gang crimes to narcotics. I am forever grateful for that experience as it allowed me to work with some of the best law enforcement officers in the country. The entire experience brought me to where I am today, which is the most fulfilling role of my career to date: opening the eyes of civilians to active shooter safety.

I was on the job when the Columbine High School shooting occurred in 1999 and watched the events unfold live on TV. As I recall, I was alone at the time, which was likely a good thing. If I hadn't been, I inevitably would've gotten questions from others such as, "Why

---

[1] "Active Shooter: How to Respond." Official Website of the Department of Homeland Security. August 22, 2018. https://www.dhs.gov/.

aren't those officers going in there?" and "Why aren't they helping those people?" At the time I simply didn't have answers to those questions.

I witnessed the police and EMS responses to the Columbine shooting and then witnessed the evaluation of their effectiveness in the aftermath. It was the beginning of major changes to come. After witnessing those events, I could no longer sit passively while more people died. I began giving presentations on active shooter response, training civilians to keep themselves alive in the event of such a tragedy.

There are a few things that I need to make perfectly clear before we go any further. When I refer to law enforcement, I'm including myself as well. Law enforcement is not perfect and never will be. We're human. We make mistakes. We learn from them and try to improve. My friends on the force were always of the utmost integrity, but I acknowledge that some officers are not. There are good people and bad people in every profession. I am not a cheerleader for law enforcement, but I want you to understand the weight of what they are required to do and the decisions they are forced to make. I am aware that most civilians have never experienced such events, and I aim to establish credibility in the form of my own experiences and observations.

In the following pages, I make reference to several active shooter events that have occurred over the years. I refer to them by venue only, and I identify the offenders in those events with the gender neutral term "shooter." I refuse to give credibility to these criminals by mentioning their name.

My approach to the topic of active shooters is reality smothered in responsibility. It is simple and driven by common sense. When someone is trying to kill you, complexities are problematic.

Twenty-four years is a long time to do anything. It's a long time to be a painter or a mechanic or a salesman; it's a really long time to be a cop. In my time as an officer, there was never a shortage of evil to be witnessed as well as the constant, methodical devaluation of human life. Every bad act seemed to have a justification component, usually presented by the offender at the time of arrest or by the offender's lawyer in court. Everyone claimed it was the fault of something or someone else, yet it was always the offender sitting there in the prison cell, whether or not the act was committed because of a bad hand dealt by life, didn't matter.

It is true that there is evil in the world, but it doesn't mean that the entire world is evil. I witnessed senseless death alongside the birth of new life. I witnessed people lose everything they had by their own careless actions, yet I also saw those who had nothing fight their way to the top by legitimate means. I learned innumerable things in those twenty-four years.

Unfortunately, people have short memories and will often repeat the same mistakes, even if it kills them. People love to say, "I won't do that again," and then they do. If you want to be safe, you have to assume that the worst can and will happen to you. Assuming the worst of people and constantly cataloguing your mistakes might seem like a dreary outlook on life, but it's all about perspective. With the exception of death itself, all of these mistakes present you with a learning opportunity. When you make a mistake or life throws you a curveball, the best thing to do is learn from it and keep swinging the bat.

All in all, I suppose I've seen a lot of bad, but I have also seen proof that the world isn't hopeless. In my twenty-four years, some of the events that stuck with me the most were the ones that made me laugh. There was one instance that I remember where the bad guy underestimated the ability of his intended victim and found himself on the wrong side of someone's fist.

While on patrol sometime in the early 1990s, I was dispatched to a fight at a high school dance in my assigned patrol area: my "beat." When I arrived, I found that the two combatants had already been separated by school staff and were sitting in different rooms. I was informed by the staff that the fight involved two boys in their early teens and was over quickly. One of the boys had temporarily lost consciousness, but had since woken up.

My role was to interview both parties and see if medical attention and criminal charges were warranted. The first young man I spoke to was the one who had lost consciousness. He was still disoriented, and I contacted an ambulance for him. His name was Tom; he was about fifteen years old, covered in gang tattoos and wearing his gang colors- black and gold, marking him as a member of a particular Chicago-based street gang. He was bleeding from his nose, and the side of his head was red, too.

According to Tom, he had been getting friendly with a young lady on the dance floor when her boyfriend, Joe, approached him and asked him to leave her alone. This angered Tom, who shot some insults at Joe and attempted to punch him in the face. Joe blocked the punch. "Then I got knocked out," Tom told me. "Well, what happened?" I questioned. "Joe kicked me in the head!"

In order for Joe to kick Tom in the head, I figured that Tom would've had to be on the ground somehow. "How did you get down on the ground to begin with?" I asked. "I wasn't on the fucking floor, I was standing there! He kicked me in the head while I was fucking standing there!" he said.

While paramedics tended to Tom, I moved on to speak to Joe in the next room. Joe was a tall, lanky kid. He was polite and respectful, but clearly shaken up over the event. "My dad's gonna kill me, my dad's gonna kill me!" he kept insisting. "I never do stuff like this!" Joe assured me that he had made every attempt to defuse the situation, but when Tom tried to strike him he defended himself. He said he'd only struck Tom once with a kick to the side of the head. One blow was enough to end the fight and there had been no need to escalate it further.

It turns out that Joe's father was a martial arts instructor and was training Joe to be a martial artist. Joe was obviously uncommonly skilled, although you would never know it by his appearance. In fact, he was so skilled that he went on to fight semi-professionally.

In this moment though, the only thing Joe could think about was his father's possible negative reaction. "I'll talk to your dad," I promised him. "You did a great job." Tom, on the other hand, was arrested in addition to getting his ass kicked.

As entertaining and inspirational as this story is for the underdog, I want you to recognize the value of it. Tom had a plan for that night at the dance. He wanted to mess with somebody, and he chose someone whom he assumed would be an easy target. Tom sought out the path of least resistance and picked someone who appeared to be a sheep. Unfortunately for Tom, Joe turned out to be a wolf in sheep's clothing. Joe was prepared for such an attack, and the fact that he countered so quickly and violently caused a disruption in Tom's plan.

It's important to remember that the attacker always has some plan or vision as to how events can unfold in his or her favor. This gives them the advantage. But as Tom and Joe's story exemplifies, an attacker can only anticipate how the intended victims will react. If the victim reacts in a way that is unexpected, the victim now has the upper hand.

This story doesn't suggest that Tom was an evil person, and it certainly doesn't mean that Tom is comparable to an active shooter. In this example, however, Tom represents the bad guy. This means that Joe can be labeled the "good guy," but as we know, the world is never that black and white. Simply having good intentions isn't enough in most circumstances. Joe was prepared and didn't hesitate to react to the threat, and this made him the victor. How does this story relate to the problem of active shooter in our world today? I want people to be prepared like Joe, and not necessarily by taking martial arts classes. Rather recently, I was watching media coverage of a shooting at the Rite Aid Distribution Center in Maryland. Hawkeye Active Shooter Response Training aims for our training and presentations to be up-to-date, so we make a point of analyzing and picking apart documented active shooter events. A witness was being interviewed in the aftermath of the shooting, and she said, "I never would have thought this could happen here."

I hear this same statement at almost every single shooting event. It amazes me that people have not yet come to the realization that shootings can and do happen everywhere. There are far too many people left feeling helpless and scared in the wake of these tragedies, which only provides more sheep for the wolves to tear apart. I want you to be prepared for an active shooter event in your school, workplace, or place of worship. I want to share with you what I've learned in my years as the police, as well as the tactics and techniques that Hawkeye Active Shooter Response continues to develop every day. There is evil in the world, and it is time for us to put it in its place.

2

Making Entry:

An analysis of how law enforcement and
EMS responses to active shooters have changed

Active shooter situations are not new. These incidents have been going on for decades, and have become even more frequent in recent years. Shooters have realized that they need to become smarter and more sophisticated, and this change seems to have begun with the Columbine High School shooting. After Columbine, people began concerning themselves with police response to active shooter events.

What made Columbine different? It was the first event of its kind to unfold on live TV. The errors made by first responders during this event were huge, and we all got to watch it on live television. The biggest problem was that law enforcement had never trained for an event like Columbine. Law enforcement has always had a very specific approach, and they were doing exactly what they had been trained to do. They were told to

a. Establish a command center

b. Establish a perimeter

c. Call for a SWAT (Special Weapons and Tactics) team

d. Establish contact with the shooter(s) to identify the demands

The problem with this system was that the shooters did not want to be contacted. They did not want to talk and had no demands; they simply wanted to kill as many people as they could before their time was up. As police set up the command center and tried to gather the SWAT team, people were being slaughtered. Thirteen people died in the Columbine shooting as a result of this system.

I am not suggesting that I would have reacted differently at the time; we only knew one way to react. But as I watched the tragedy unfold along with the rest of the world, I thought, "This plan is just not working."

Columbine was the flint that started the spark of change. At first, it was law enforcement tactics and approach that were altered. Officers would no longer stand by waiting to establish a command center and anticipating the arrival of the SWAT team. Initially, after patrol units were armed with more appropriate gear and weapons for an active shooter event, they would gather in groups of three to four officers. That team would then methodically enter the scene and seek out the threat. We soon discovered that this method was also insufficient, as waiting to make entry was causing loss of life. In recent years, law enforcement response has been modified yet again. Now the first officer on the scene makes entry - alone if necessary - and addresses the threat. This solo method creates a new dynamic that requires different training and a partnership with EMS personnel.

More than just physical training, officers must also train their minds to override their fear. Yes; fear. Police officers are extremely well-trained individuals, but they are human beings and fear cannot be trained out of a person. Such an idea may come as a surprise, as police officers often seem fearless.

But police work is no comic book. Officers are not invincible, and flying bullets are terrifying. Police are the only ones running towards the gunfire in these situations instead of running away from it, and there is nothing fun about it. We have even seen instances where training is not effective enough and fear takes over, preventing the officer from properly doing his or her job. Police are faced with a "kill or be killed" decision that must be made in seconds amidst thoughts of "Will I ever see my family again?" and "How bad does being shot actually hurt?"

Police get scared, and they know that even if they come out of the shooting alive, they cannot win. Their methods will be criticized and second guessed the next day by civilians and by the media. At times, they cannot even count on their own administration or employer to support them. I recognize that mistakes are sometimes made and people need to be held accountable for those mistakes, especially when lives are at stake. That's a lot to think about when you're trying to save innocent lives as well as your own in mere seconds.

When I was a Patrol Sergeant many years ago, there was an active shooter event in a neighboring town. We shared a radio network with multiple other police agencies. Finding airtime could be difficult, but there was also no shortage of assistance if you needed it. We knew each other's business and had each other's back. This particular incident took place post-Columbine, after some of the new training methods had been implemented. When the first calls came in regarding an active shooter, all other radio traffic stopped and deployment of resources began immediately. At this point in my career, I was no longer actively participating on the High Risk Entry Team (our department's version of a SWAT team). Instead, I was the watch commander for my shift that day, meaning I had the responsibility of directing officers under my command.

The SWAT team had received notification of the event, but it would be over long before they would arrive. I dispatched one of our officers to assist the other agency, and multiple officers from different departments arrived on the scene simultaneously. Upon arrival, officers reported being able to hear gunfire coming from inside the facility. I was monitoring the situation and radio traffic from our agency's dispatch center. I heard every word and hung on every transmission, but I was most concerned with what my dispatched officer was doing and what actions he would take. He was my primary responsibility.

The officers were following their usual trained response to an active shooter event; they established a perimeter and confirmed that the SWAT team was on the way. All radio inquiries and commands occurred in seconds. But officers were also beginning to somewhat implement the solo approach, and as such I heard the voice of the single officer I had dispatched say, "I hear gunfire inside. I'm making entry."

I quickly responded with "10-4", ultimately giving him my permission to enter the building and do what needed to be done. He was immediately followed by several other officers who had the same task and intention, but none had any idea what they were walking into. The shooter had fired multiple rounds while searching for his estranged girlfriend. He was driving around inside the facility in a vehicle he had commandeered, firing out of the window. A few minutes later, the event was over. The shooter took his own life. By God's grace, the shooter was the only casualty.

It's likely that the shooter knew the police were closing in on him when he ended his life. The newly trained quick response undoubtedly played a role in this final outcome, and lives were saved as a result. This strategy did not come without great risk and fear. My officer was afraid to go in there, and I was afraid to send him. The fact that the shooter did not hurt nor hit anyone was nothing short of a miracle, and the outcome certainly would have been much different if not for the officers' quick response.

This shooting lasted about ten minutes from start to finish. Ten minutes might not seem like a lot of time… until someone is trying to kill you. As per usual in the aftermath of such an incident, we analyzed and critiqued our own police response. What could we have done better or faster? How could we improve what we had done in order to save more lives? We came to the conclusion that we had performed more quickly and efficiently than we had ever done in the past. As always, communication could have been better, but we were generally pleased with the improvements. Debriefs are an important part of assessing the outcome of police response. In such a setting, rank supposedly doesn't matter, allowing police to openly express their thoughts without fear of repercussions. Although the verbal discussions were not always revolutionary, they tended to provoke the thoughts of just a few people, and sometimes that is enough.

Police work as a whole takes a lot of training. It requires training for speculative scenarios that rarely (or never) occur during an officer's career. An officer must learn to place public safety above his own, and do so professionally and flawlessly. Training tirelessly is the best way for anyone to learn how to anticipate and react to these dangerous situations. It's more than just running drills and ensuring your physical capability in high stress events. Non-police are not necessarily in prime physical condition, and I recognize this. It's not just about winning against an active shooter on a physical "battlefield"; there is a fight against fear to be won inside your own head, too. For police, hands-on training usually only occurs once a month, but running through mental scenarios becomes a daily exercise.

We initially referred to this method as *If - Then Thinking*. If this happens, then I must react in this way. The method eventually became known as *When - Then Thinking*. With the increasing amount of such events, it was no longer a question of *if*, but a question of *when*.

Let me tell you honestly that this technique saved my ass on more than one occasion. It works. When you start using this mental self-training technique, you come to realize how little time it takes for destructive actions and reparative reactions to occur. The water moves from still and calm to a chaotic rip current in the blink of an eye. You must learn to react to threats that materialize out of thin air. Once a police officer figures out how to save himself in these situations, he is reminded of his oath of office. He serves the public, and they are the ones who need to be saved first. "But," he wonders, "How can I save them first if I don't know that they need help until they call me?" Not every life-threatening occurrence begins with an explosion that can be seen from miles away. First responders don't always know that they need to rush to the scene to save people. I love action movies as much as the next person, but real life doesn't work that way. In many cases, an officer could be right outside the building of a horrific event and not be aware of it until somebody on the inside of the building makes them aware. These are the realities of such events.

Causing people harm has been a crime since time immemorial, and police emerged as a way to ensure that fewer people were harmed. Crime has never been sensible or justifiable, but in the past, criminals typically had reasons for committing crime. Now there is a terrifying new threat in the world of crime; criminals are killing just for the sake of killing and creating carnage. Understanding these destructive actions is becoming impossible. Some of these events may be predictable, but most of them leave us with unanswered questions, turning us into intended victims trapped like deer in headlights. People wonder, "If the police are supposed to keep us safe, then why aren't they doing it? Why is this happening?"

As I mentioned earlier, post-incident debriefs are vital opportunities for police officers to set aside their rank and egos and learn from their mistakes. Real lessons are often buried in what a person is thinking rather than saying, and none of us were willing to verbalize what we were really thinking about that active shooter event. We knew that we had already made significant changes to our method of active shooter response, and that it was an improvement over what we had done in the past. But no matter how much we changed and improved, we were still reacting to an event that was already in progress. People were being killed, and we weren't preventing anything. Despite this unspoken realization, it would be years before law enforcement would readily admit the truth to themselves and even longer before they would verbalize that realization to the public. We were just never going to get there in time.

3

A State of Mind:

Rewiring the universal complacency and
fear associated with active shooter

We all know that our mistakes can teach us powerful life lessons, but sometimes it's easier to learn from the mistakes of other people than from our own. It tends to be less painful, as any younger sibling knows from watching their older siblings. As a civilian and witness to active shooter events through TV and media, you can learn from the mistakes of police and other civilians in regards to active shooter response. Sometimes the solution lies in learning to deprogram our false notions and pay more attention to the obvious. In order to respond properly to active shooter events, you must apprehend them at face value instead of letting the media and the opinions of others twist the realities of these tragedies.

If you talk to anyone old enough to remember the events of 9/11, they will be able to tell you where they were and what they were doing when the terrorist attack took place. Even those who can't remember the attack itself relive the tragedy every year on the anniversary of that date. I was on duty the morning of the attacks, and when the first plane struck the North Tower, I was in a local convenience store. I would stop there every morning, say hello to the owner, and grab a cup of coffee. That morning, the store owner told me what had happened, and only minutes afterwards, all units on the street were summoned to the police station for an emergency meeting. We were just as shocked and helpless as everyone else as we watched the news coverage. We wanted to help; we were first responders after all, and that was our job. But we were hundreds of miles away, and there was nothing we could do to help the victims of that tragedy. The most horrifying part was that it didn't seem like the fire, police, and EMS personnel in New York City could do much, either.

No plan, no strategy, no tactics, and no technology could help them in that moment. As we tried to wrap our heads around the atrocities we were seeing, we realized that even trained first responders were not trained to handle anything like this. There was only one difference between law enforcement and every other person who witnessed the events of 9/11. We were forced to shake it off, acknowledge what had happened, clear our heads, and get to work. We had to do something. Anything. We couldn't help at Ground Zero, but we had our own mass of civilians looking to us for answers. We had no real plan, but we developed an approach of high visibility and maintaining order so that things didn't erupt into chaos. We went to local schools to assure students and staff that, for the moment, our little corner of the world was okay. Parents were rushing through the doors of the schools to get their kids and figure out what to do next. One teacher met me at the front door, tears streaming down her face.

She asked me, "Are we at war?"

I could only say, "I don't know."

What could I say to console her? We were no better prepared for that day than anybody else. The only thing we could do in the aftermath was let people know that we were still out there.

If ever there was an event in my lifetime that generated true change in public awareness, it was 9/11. There are lessons to be learned from every tragedy, and 9/11 brought us the realization that the world is capable of far greater tragedies than we might expect. It forced us to understand that bad things happen to good people, and that tragedies strike anywhere and at any time. As a country, we had all been asleep at the wheel. We had relied upon someone or something else to take care of us: some alert system, government entity, or first responder. But for the first time, people began looking over their shoulders and wondering, "Am I alone in this?"

In the face of such a tragedy, this was a great lesson. The United States began to unite with one common purpose, and people had a newfound love for their country. Maybe we were alone, but we were alone together. As a first responder, cop, and trained observer, I saw people opening their eyes for the first time.

Even when people learn powerful lessons, they tend to forget. People have short memories. They get easily wrapped up in daily life, becoming comfortable, complacent, and ultimately vulnerable. As first responders, we make it our business to remember those lessons and to improve ourselves, but civilians just wanted to get back to normal as quickly as possible. When I was in high school, I took two years of German. I was never fluent, but I knew enough to get by. Since then, I have had few opportunities to use the language and as such, I recall almost nothing from those years of lessons. I can still recognize German if I hear it, but if I had practiced the grammar and vocabulary on a regular basis, I would be fluent enough to speak it if the need presented itself.

Any skill takes practice. Training yourself to recognize and react to dangerous situations requires a certain mindset that, like fluency in a language, cannot be turned on and off whenever you need it. 9/11 was a terrible tragedy, and most of us can't even imagine the pain suffered by those who lost friends and family members in the attacks. Out of respect for those who were lost, and for the future safety of our country, we cannot take the lessons learned lightly. It is not enough to say, "There are lessons to be learned here." What are those lessons? How can you apply them to your everyday life?

Many years ago, I arrested a young man for theft. He was a 24-year old heroin addict stealing to support his habit, and already had a lengthy criminal history. I had arrested him a few years previously when I was a gang crimes officer and he'd been involved with a local street gang.

The arrestee was in his cell, and I was sitting out of eyeshot doing paperwork. He called me over and instructed me, "There's a TAC officer, his name is Dan. Dan Sko-something. Call him. Call him and he'll tell you that I'm a good guy. I helped him out years ago on some cases. He knows me!"

His mind was so damaged by the drugs that he couldn't even recognize me.

I played along. "Yea, I'm not sure who you're talking about."

"He used to be a gang guy. Dan Sko-something."

"I'll try and reach out for him," I said, "but he works a different shift and I don't see him very often. If I can get ahold of him, I'll see what he thinks of you."

I came back to the cell an hour later and brought him something to eat.

"Did you get ahold of Officer Dan?" he wanted to know.

I told him I had. "I talked to him about you. He treated you fairly way back when and gave you plenty of breaks, but you haven't cleaned up your act. But he wishes you well and hopes you do better later in life."

Eventually we began to have a conversation with a little more meaning. He told me that his parents were divorced. His dad was gone most of the time and his mom was always working, leaving him to fend for himself. He had moved from one school to another until he finally stopped going altogether and dropped out. He'd had a difficult time making friends, ended up with the wrong crowd, and it was all downhill from there.

The story was familiar. I'd heard it too many times before, and it wasn't much different from my own. The difference lies in blame. This man chose to blame everyone else for his current situation. His parents were divorced, but so were mine and countless others. They didn't make him start using heroin. He did that. He'd walked a long and tough road in life to end up in that jail cell, but he got himself there and he would have to get himself out. His parents weren't the ones sitting in a jail cell; he was. He just couldn't take responsibility for his own actions.

If there's one thing I want you to learn from that heroin addict, it's this: You are responsible for you. Eventually, we all become old dogs, and you don't have to be old to be one; it's a state of mind, a state of complacency. The only way to stay sharp and to stay alive is by learning new tricks. It's your responsibility to seek out the resources you need to learn those tricks. The first step is simple: Look in the mirror and tell yourself, "I can do this." Reset your state of mind. After that, I'll help you apply your new state of mind to active shooter response. Following the events of 9/11 when first responders were forced to learn new tricks, I came to the realization that everyone could benefit from learning these simplistic methods and tactics.

4

There's an App for That:

A look at the over-reliance on technology
to solve problems

From time to time, I am contacted by a tech company that claims to have the solution to the active shooter problem. I've been presented with many ideas for applications. Some approaches are similar and focus on summoning help, while others are unique, designed to incapacitate the shooter in some way. There is one factor that all of these proposed solutions have in common: none of them are the "be all and end all" in regards to active shooter response. A few showed promise, but an app would not have made much difference in the Las Vegas Mandalay Bay shooting. With the gunman opening fire from the window of a hotel room over throngs of people, he had the advantage. The concertgoers were fish in a barrel. Help did indeed arrive quickly; it just wasn't enough and implementing an app wouldn't have changed anything.

Many of these tech solutions offer an enhancement of safety in an active shooter incident. That may help in some respects, but it also presents an inherent risk that then goes unrecognized. If you let yourself believe that pressing a button or pulling an alarm box will save you in an active shooter event, you have already undone the mindset we established in the last chapter. You've once again signed up to be a victim reliant on someone else to save you. These would-be victims are like sheep; easily herded, mindlessly following whoever is in front of them. They have no independent thought processes and only know how to follow the masses.

We have become a society that demands instant gratification. All things should be at our fingertips with the touch of a button or the swipe of a screen. I admit that technology can be a blessing (if it's working properly and you know how to use it). The problem is that it does not always work properly, and is oftentimes defeated by the simplest errors.

Back when I was still on the police department, we responded to a bank robbery call. It was one of those banks that set up shop inside a large grocery store chain. The call came in seconds after the robber had fled the store. Fortunately, we had squad cars in the immediate area. The caller informed our dispatch center that the bank had utilized loss prevention technology by inserting an exploding dye pack into the bundle of currency stolen by the offender. Dye packs are relatively simple. After a trigger on the pack is activated, it bursts open, spewing out a red dye and emitting smoke that stains everything it encounters. The dye would therefore ruin the currency and typically stain the offender's skin, clothing, and vehicle.

At this point in our story, the bad guy had run behind a nearby strip mall and was met by several responding officers. He had already stuffed the stolen money- and unknowingly, the dye pack- in his front pocket. There was a foot pursuit, which only lasted about 60 seconds before the dye pack burst. Red dye covered the man's upper body and face, yet he still continued to run with determination. The distance between the robber and the officers began to grow as the officers struggled to catch their breath- not from the chase itself but from laughing at the plume of red smoke running off into the distance. There was only one guy screaming, emitting red smoke from his pants, and running through yards, so catching him was relatively easy after that. He tried to hide under a deck in a residential area, where he continued to smolder and give off smoke signals until we arrived and pulled him out.

Technology did play a role in solving that crime. The dye pack was fairly simple and easy to deploy, which is what made it effective. Fast forward a few years and the same bank was robbed again. Because technology advances so rapidly, the bank had since abandoned the dye pack for a GPS tracking unit, a flat device that was also concealed within the stolen currency. The GPS unit was supposed to produce a signal that would appear as a map on a screen at the police department. The dispatch center would then tell responding officers where to find the stolen money and the offender or offenders. Unfortunately, there was a problem. We received the signal, but with a two minute delay. The GPS unit was also more difficult to conceal than the dye pack. If the bad guy looked closely at the bundle of bills, he'd know he was being tracked.

It wasn't long before the GPS stopped moving and appeared to be only a few blocks away from the bank. We were optimistic, quickly setting up our perimeter around the area and flooding it with officers from several assisting departments. We couldn't see anyone nearby, but there was a possibility that the offenders had dropped the stolen cash or some other evidence. The area was compact and wild grass covered, but not so thick that you couldn't see through to the pond in the middle of it. We searched for thirty to forty-five minutes, but it became increasingly obvious that the GPS was at the bottom of the pond. We were back to square one with our investigation and now the offender had a significant time and distance advantage over us.

Both the bank and law enforcement assumed that new technology would make the investigation smoother and easier, yet it became detrimental in the face of reality. Simply put, the bad guys wanted the money. They may not have recognized the GPS unit when they found it, but it had no value to them and was promptly discarded. If we compare the outcomes of these two robberies, the simpler of the two technologies was the most successful. I acknowledge that technology does have benefits, but I want to point out its faults so we do not continue to let it think for us.

We have all experienced the dreaded computer or network crash; the whole world seems to stop until the internet starts functioning again. Our expectation of instant gratification has turned us into a society of button-pushers. We're all reaching for the Staples Easy Button. When we want groceries or clothes, we go online, click a button, and it's delivered to our doors, erasing the thought process formerly required to perform basic tasks. But if you push the Easy Button and nothing happens, would you know what to do? Many of us would push it again, praying for a different result.

When someone is trying to kill you- when you are in the heat of the moment- you'll be lucky if you can remember your own name, let alone where that button is. If you're fortunate enough to actually push the button, you're then left waiting for someone to swoop in and save you- the distressed caller on the other end of Batman's Batphone.

In the case of an active shooter situation, technology may aid you in indicating your need for assistance, but it will not save you.

Relying on an alarm system or button allows you to settle into complacency and feel comforted by a false sense of security. You could quite possibly be found dead with your finger on the button, still waiting for help to arrive. Technology, with its tendency to fail at the worst of times, is not a reliable solution to this problem. Yes, someday there may be an app for that. But what if on the day you need it, the day your life depends on it, you have no signal or a dead battery on your phone?

5

The Value of Common Sense:

Understanding the importance of a basic and
instinctual action plan under extreme stress

Research, statistics and analytics have their place and their
value. By studying past events and missteps, we learn how to correct
our mistakes and perhaps prevent similar ones in the future. Yet
sometimes the only answer that matters in the midst of an event is the
one that is instinctual and keeps you alive. Perhaps while we continue
to search for the cure to the disease that is the active shooter epidemic,
we should focus on minimizing its impact.

It's almost reminiscent of another desperate attempt to cure
something: the common cold. Scientists, studied, researched, and
analyzed for decades. Ultimately, they came to the conclusion that
preventing the spread of the virus was easier than curing it, which is
best achieved by merely washing one's hands.

Humans are supposed to be the superior race, which we
rationalize to ourselves by how easily we're able to acquire knowledge
and apply it to create change. Unfortunately, when it comes to our
survival instincts, this need to acquire an explanation works to our
detriment. After all, we are animals just like God's other creations, and
He gave us certain instincts intended to protect us from harm. By
rationalizing ourselves away from our instincts, we deprogram our
safety precautions and replace them with "intelligence."

In order to understand our relationship to our survival instincts, let's take a closer look at predators and prey in nature. What can we learn from their successes and ability to survive? It's not that animals can't learn; they can and they do. Their application of learned skills is sometimes nothing short of amazing. But their life and their existence is kept simple. They sleep when they're tired. They hunt when they're hungry and drink when they're thirsty. They mate to maintain their species, they're always aware of their surroundings in order to avoid becoming prey, and that's the extent of their lifestyle. They don't over-complicate things and instead stick to their instincts. When it comes to survival, humans can't hold a candle to animals.

When we first established Hawkeye Active Shooter Response, the hawk was an obvious front runner for our logo. A hawk sees everything. Sneaking up on a hawk and causing it harm is not an easy task, and when it's time to fight, the hawk is a formidable opponent. This bird of prey is a hunter and a survivor, constantly alert. When was the last time you saw a hawk distracted by anything? Such an animal embodies many of the elements that we want to teach our students about awareness and response, and thus it became our symbol.

In addition to the hawk, the rattlesnake is another animal that knows when and how to fight. If you have ever been unfortunate enough to encounter one of these vipers in the wild, it's an experience you won't quickly forget. What's interesting is that the rattlesnake doesn't see you as their prey; in reality, they want to be left alone and will generally go out of their way to get away from you. But if you're stupid enough to pursue one and corner it, you will not find it hiding face-first with its head under a rock. The snake has anticipated that you might pursue it and when you get there, it's ready and waiting for you. Its attack is lightning fast and deadly, yet the process of awareness is instinctual and requires little thought for the snake.

Humans tend to over-complicate things, and when panic sets in, we can't remember what we've spent so much time studying and learning. When someone is trying to kill you, you do not want your instincts suppressed by your own learned perceptions. Your instincts are there to save you! Sometimes you just can't explain away the obvious with books, studies, statistics, and theories.

As I write this, I'm reminded of an incident that occurred when I was in sixth grade. Our sixth grade teacher was discussing multiplication, and he told us that the total of any number multiplied by zero is zero. We agreed, since this had been taught to us in earlier years and was accepted as fact. The teacher invited one of the students to the front of the class and handed him three oranges from his desk. He then said he was going to multiply those three oranges by the value of zero. Based on what we had been taught, the answer to the math problem was zero. But what of the three oranges? The oranges didn't disappear- they were still there. We had a good laugh about it, but nobody had an acceptable explanation. You can't make a physical object vanish, regardless of the facts of math. Intellect gives us the mathematical answer of zero, but common sense tells us that we can still see the oranges.

When you're confronted with an active shooter situation or any violent type of encounter, you have to keep the brain from going into overload and shutting down. Police refer to this phenomenon as "condition black", but it's also known as "deer in headlights syndrome." It takes precious seconds for the brain to rationalize and process what is going on around you, but the time that it takes to rationalize could cost you your life. But you can program yourself with an instinctual reaction so you don't have to waste time rationalizing. When someone sneaks up behind you and startles you, you jump on reflex, and you should have a similar reaction when confronted with the sound of gunfire. Jump to action. Keep a clear head. Implement the plan that you already have established.

It sounds simple- too simple- but if someone is trying to kill you, it will be difficult to recall anything you've read in this book unless it's something simple, applicable, and instinctual. For those of you who are readers, I recommend a book by Gavin DeBecker called *The Gift of Fear*.[1] The book, written by a behavioral analyst, is about the importance of fear and is supported by real stories. Fear is a gift, an instinct. It exists to keep us safe from harm. Sometimes we fear certain ideas with such intensity that we begin to suppress those fears that trigger our survival instincts. We elect to ignore the threat presented by active shooter to the point that we are completely unprepared for it to happen, yet we lie awake at night worried about a presentation for work. You have to ask yourself: which of those two is a matter of life and death?

---

[1] DeBecker, Gavin. *The Gift of Fear*. London: Bloomsbury, 2000.

6

When Seconds Count,

the Police Are Only Minutes Away:

A realistic look at the "Man in the Red Cape" theory

It's time to cut to the chase here. No one wants to see active shooter events occur, but they still happen, and someone has to train to prevent them. The police are hard-working men and women who would lay down their lives to protect people that they've never met. The job can be thankless, which is why it's important to recognize that police officers are also human. Though well-intended, they cannot work miracles. When we ask the police to respond to such a fast-paced event and to take action, we ask the impossible. They cannot get there in time to save everybody. To further dispel the theory that someone will swoop in and save you - the "Man in the Red Cape" theory - let's break down how an active shooter event might unfold.

Seconds, not minutes, save lives in these events. Statistically, a person is shot every fifteen seconds once the shooting starts until the offender is stopped. But exactly how long will it take for help to arrive? To create a hypothetical scenario, imagine that a shooter enters a facility. He is intent on doing as much harm as possible before it's all over. The shooter produces his weapon and fires a round into his first intended victim. The first victim is killed instantly. The clock is running. The first shot was heard by several other would-be victims but they're not certain what the sound was, so they move toward the gunfire to further investigate. Several more shots ring out and several more victims are killed. Those that are not hit or are only wounded in the second barrage of gunfire are now certain of danger and begin to scramble about. Some begin to yell and scream. Others say nothing as they try to convince themselves of what is actually happening. *Nothing like this could ever happen here,* they think. As those initial intended victims flee and scream, more people begin to recognize the level of danger they're in.

At a minimum of one to two minutes into the event, no one has even called 911 yet.

Remember that one person is being shot every fifteen seconds. In the chaos, several people are able to get out of the building. Others hide in closets, bathrooms or under a desk.

Two to three minutes into the event, someone is able to call 911 from a cell phone.

The 911 dispatcher answers with "911, where is your emergency?" The call is coming from a cell phone, making the exact location of the caller unclear. The primary goal of the 911 operator is to figure out where the caller is before asking what's going on. The caller is in panic mode. They have worked in this facility for the past five years, but now they can't even remember the address. The caller hears gunshots getting closer, and falls silent out of fear of giving away their position to the shooter. Four to five minutes into the incident and the police have still not been dispatched.

Not to worry; by this time, others have escaped the building and they too are calling 911. In fact, seven or eight of them are all calling at the same time. Others have called family and friends to inform them of what is happening. Family and friends also call 911. The media has heard that something big is going on and they also begin to call the police station to get further details. The emergency dispatch center becomes overloaded and calls are disconnected. 911 lines or "trunks" can only handle so many calls at once. While it's important not to overwhelm the 911 operator, if you can make the call to 911 from a landline, do so. The operator will know where the call came from and dispatch officers to investigate.

Five to six minutes into the event and the first officers are dispatched to the scene.

Response times to these events have improved dramatically over the years, but as of November 2018, the national average for the first officers to arrive on scene is about six minutes. If four people are shot every minute, twenty-four have already been shot by the time the police arrive at the front door. Notice that I said "at the front door." They still need to get into the building, search for and locate the offender(s), and terminate the threat. That process may take several additional minutes due to the current chaos. Meanwhile, the shooter continues to rack up the body count. It's easy to see how an incident that only lasts a few minutes can produce so many casualties.

Truth be told, most of these events are over before the police can arrive on the scene. Many end with the shooter taking his or her own life. The footage of these tragedies on TV shows us a lot of police activity and presence, but it usually occurs after the fact when it's too late. Once law enforcement came to terms with the fact that they could not rescue people fast enough or without help, changes were implemented. At first, "change" meant police could no longer wait for the SWAT team to assemble, plan their approach and entry, and methodically search the building. Instead, patrol officers were appropriately armed with shoulder mounted weapons and trained to use those weapons. Patrol units would be the first units responding to the scene, ideally within minutes of receiving a call. If we could quickly assemble a unit of four officers, appropriately armed and trained to make entry, we would save more lives. While this course of thinking was correct in that a quicker entry would save more lives, it still required us to wait for four officers to arrive at the scene and make entry. The approach was tactically sound with the aim to outman and outgun the threat, but the flaw was time.

Today, the first officer to arrive on scene is expected to make entry and seek out the threat, armed with whatever is at their disposal (although most are appropriately prepared). With the first officer entering the spider's lair, he or she must rely on his or her training and press on with the reassurance that back-up officers are minutes away. The current mandates and protocols place officers at risk of life and limb to do their job, but they have taken an oath to protect the lives of others. Despite their fears, they must press on.

It's important to understand police response because it will help you formulate your own response. You must understand what first responders are dealing with when they arrive so you're not accidentally hurt by them. They're running into the most chaotic event they've ever seen. People are running everywhere, yelling and screaming, crying and pointing. The radio is barking out small bits of information into their ear every second, and they have to decide which pieces are important and accurate in that moment. In the midst of everything, they are searching for and trying to isolate the individual with the gun. There could only be one individual, but there might be two, three, or even more. If the police see a concealed carry holder with a gun in such a situation, or if a civilian took the gun from the shooter, that person may be seen as a potential threat. Police are there to terminate the threat, so don't make yourself look like one.

Recently, EMS has been working more closely with law enforcement in active shooter situations. The Rescue Task Force (RTF), for example, is comprised of both EMS and law enforcement. The RTF makes entry immediately after the event, meaning they're no longer afforded the luxury of waiting until the scene is secured before they go in and tend to the injured. Their response is similar to that which you would see on a battlefield. Their objective is to get injured parties transported to a hospital as quickly as possible for treatment, not to treat them on scene. A gunshot victim's probability of survival increases greatly if they arrive at the hospital quickly. EMS is on a mission of recovery and transport, and they will dive into the fray wearing bulletproof vests in order to save people. The aim of EMS is to recover and transport as quickly as possible. The police will walk past injured individuals in pursuit of their mission. Until the scene is secured you may find yourself forced to tend to your own injuries and it is imperative that you are prepared to do so.

Unfortunately, as I write this book, new active shooters events occur and emerge daily. Prior to writing this chapter, there was yet another senseless mass shooting in a synagogue in Pennsylvania. Apparently, targets were selected by the lone shooter based on their religious beliefs. Eleven innocent people perished and several others were injured. The shooter was not challenged until the police arrived and were able to return fire, incapacitating the shooter. The event lasted twenty minutes. Despite the fact that eleven people were killed, it is nothing short of a miracle that there were not more. Remember: A victim is typically shot every fifteen seconds until the shooter is stopped. I'm not suggesting that you raise your hand to be a hero; I'm suggesting that you refuse to raise your hand to be a victim. Here's some key points to remember:[1]

- Run when you can. If you are not responsible for anybody in the building except for yourself, then do what you can to get out. If the shooter can see you, you're too close.

- Hide if running is not an option. This may be the case if you either have no path of egress or because you are responsible for others in the building that you have chosen to help.

- Fight if you must. Fight for your life, because your life depends on it. Fighting an individual armed with a gun may seem difficult, but if there is one gun and two people are fighting for control over it, the victor is the one who maintains control in the end. The only dangerous part of the gun is the muzzle (the end that the projectile comes out of). Maintain control and keep the muzzle pointed down and away from you. Once you have control of the gun in such a fashion, there are no rules. That person is trying to kill you and you are trying to survive. The fight is not intended to be fair and the winner is the one who walks away in the end.

In Thousand Oaks California at a local bar, a shooter took the lives of twelve innocent individuals. In the face of such tragedy, it's important to learn from the mistakes that were made, and this event brings up some points that relate to this particular chapter. The first officer responding to the Thousand Oaks call was shot and killed upon

---

[1] "Active Shooter." Citizen Corps | Ready.gov. https://www.ready.gov/active-shooter.

entering the building. The officer's immediate backup helped his downed comrade and retreated, waiting for additional officers to arrive on the scene. By the time additional backup arrived, the shooter had taken his own life and the event was over.

Even if the police have arrived on scene, it doesn't mean you are saved. If the shooter is still active and engaging with law enforcement, those few seconds may actually be more dangerous. Who, then, is responsible for saving you?

7

Lives and Livelihoods:

Addressing the liabilities and responsibilities
of the companies involved in active shooter events

     Many people ask "who is responsible" for an active shooter event, but it might be better to break that responsibility into pieces. In an active shooter scenario, fingers start pointing before the shooting has even stopped, and there is usually plenty of blame to go around. The first person to be blamed is, of course, the shooter himself. This appears obvious, but in many cases, the shooter does not survive the event. If the shooter does survive the event, he'll spend the rest of his days in prison. Neither the victims nor the families of the victims are likely to receive any sort of compensation from the shooter.

     In the aftermath, the two entities most frequently sued are:
- The first responders
- The venue where the event occurred

     The venue and the first responders' agencies are more likely to produce a settlement that is compensating to the survivors. In a July 2, 2013 court decision from Hennepin County, Minnesota, the court found that the employer, Accent Signage, was liable for negligence and failure to train their employees. The civil case was filed by the victim's family members in response to an active shooter incident that had occurred at the place of business on September 27, 2012. Andrew Engeldinger, a company employee, entered Accent Signage armed with a pistol. Once inside, Engeldinger shot and killed numerous employees before killing himself. During the proceedings, the shooter's estate was released from liability. The employer was held liable for failure to train and for failure to recognize the indicators of the potential threat.[1]

The one commonality amongst all of these tragic events is people. People are the shooters and the cause of these horrific events, but they also have the potential to be the solution. It is the actions or inactions of people that put these events in motion, and it is the actions of people that will provide the solution.

In yet another case, the estates of two of the students killed in the Sandy Hook School shooting incident in December 2012 filed suit against the Town of Newtown and its Board of Education. The lawsuit alleges insufficient security on school grounds but also cites failure to train and supervise the staff for lockdown and evacuation plans.[2] This particular lawsuit was brought by the estates of only two of the students that were killed, so there were likely other pending civil actions on behalf of the other eighteen students and six adults. In the aftermath of an active shooter event, there is no shortage of liability to go around. The employer can be held liable under negligent hiring for not checking the shooter's criminal history, especially considering the accessibility of the information, and for placing him in a position conducive to crime. The employer is also responsible under the OSHA General Duty Clause for not training its employees to react to a recognizable hazard in the workplace. The employer is responsible not

---

[1] Deborah A. Beneke, Trustee for the Heirs and Next Kin of Jacob B. Beneke, deceased, vs. Accent Signage Systems, Inc. and The Estate of Andrew J. Engeldinger, individually. Case No. 27-CV-13-1268. (District Court February 1, 2013).

[2] Scinto, Rich, and Patch Staff. "Sandy Hook Shooting Lawsuit: Town Asks Judge To Toss Case." Stone Mountain-Lithonia, GA Patch. July 04, 2017. https://patch.com.

only for the families of the victims losing a loved one, but also the possible loss of a means of income.

If you are an employer, owner, manager or director of a company, you are responsible for your employees. You are responsible for recognizing and acknowledging the threat, and choosing to train and prepare your employees. It is absolutely vital to develop policies and procedures that provide resources for their protection. The OSHA Act of 1970 General Duty Clause requires employers to maintain workplaces "free from recognized hazards that are causing or are likely to cause death or serious physical harm."[1] Is there anything that fits this definition more than an active shooter? It would appear that the courts are in agreement, as recent court rulings relative to liability lawsuits have shown that active shooter scenarios are now considered a "recognizable hazard" to employees. It is as much about saving livelihoods as it is about saving lives. No one is ever going to completely prevent these events from occurring, but we can mitigate the impact. We can mitigate the loss of life as well as the financial impact and downtime that the company sustains as the result of becoming a crime scene. We can mitigate the chance that the workplace in question ceases to exist as a result of the tragedy. In the examples cited above, the lack of preparation left the defendants open to countless losses and liabilities, most notably the loss of human life. Employers who fail to protect their employees may be liable.

- Jury awards for inadequate security suits average $1.2 million nationwide and settlements average $600,000[2]

---

[1] "OSHA Laws & Regulations." Occupational Safety and Health Administration. https://www.osha.gov.
[2] "7 Reasons Employers Should Address Domestic Violence." Futures Without Violence. August 25, 2014. https://www.futureswithoutviolence.org.

- The average cost of a single workplace homicide incident is $800,000[1]
- About 500,000 victims of violent crime in the workplace lose an estimated 1.8 million workdays each year[2]
- The average cost to American businesses each year is estimated to be $36 billion dollars[3]

Our main priority in an active shooter event is to survive, but we also can't lose sight of the survival of the business in which the event occurred. You want to make sure you'll have a business to return to when the dust finally settles on the event.

As I mentioned, the first responders and their employing agencies may be held liable in addition to the venue. There may be claims that the first responders did not get there fast enough, or did not act appropriately when they had contact with the shooter. In the weeks that follow the shooting, the friends and family of the shooter will be assessed some level of responsibility. There will likely be cries of, "Somebody should have seen this coming" or "Someone should have done or said something." Ultimately, each part of the system owns a piece of the blame.

The shooter has the advantage of walking through the door with a plan and a high level of conviction. The criminals that commit these acts are also committed to the fact that they will not survive. While we will never prevent these events entirely, we can disrupt the shooter's plan by having a plan of our own. The shooter anticipates his

---

[1] National Institute for Occupational Safety and Health.
[2] Bureau of Justice Statistics.
[3] Ibid.

victims to be fish in a barrel, so we cannot be fish. We must not wait to die in a barrel.

8

Be the Hero of Your Own Story:

How to save yourself using imagery
and a warrior state of mind

"Who is going to save me?" If you have not yet answered this question on your own, if you have not yet figured it out throughout the course of this book, I will now divulge the secret to your survival in an active shooter event: Your survival depends on you. There's just not enough time in these events for any other solution to be plausible. You are going to have to save yourself.

Many of you may think, "I would be paralyzed by fear" and "There's no way I could defend myself." I'm telling you that this is not true. People are naturally equipped with the skills they need to save themselves. You have energy inside you that is designed to be explosive when you need it. You simply need to keep the cork on the bottle, shake it, and pop the cork when the time comes.

The key is in the preparation. I'm not talking about going to the gym, taking a self-defense course, or even getting your concealed carry permit and training at the range. These are all great steps and individual choices, but it takes a certain level of commitment to see the true benefits. If you're committed enough, it'll be beneficial, but it's still not the preparation that I'm talking about. Over the years, I have been taught some of the most incredible police and self-defense tactics. I've studied numerous martial arts disciplines and trained with some of the best instructors, but that's still not the preparation I'm talking about. Every battle is won in the mind before you engage the enemy. Henry Ford once said, "Whether you think you can or you think you can't, you're probably right."

During my career in law enforcement and as a trainer and public speaker, I've had the pleasure of meeting some incredible people who've been placed in life-threatening situations and rose to the occasion to save themselves. Some of these folks were well-trained for the events, and others just happened to be there. A couple of years ago I met a young lady named Samantha. Samantha was a Human Resources Agent working for a company that had chosen to participate in Hawkeye Active Shooter Response. We conducted some scenario-based training for their employees at several facilities, located in three different states.

One component of that training is an overall assessment of the facility for safety and security as pertains to the preservation of life during an active shooter event. During the course of the tour, Samantha and I discussed the importance of trauma kits in the workplace, what those kits should contain, and where they should be located. I mentioned that many people do not even know what a tourniquet is, let alone how to apply it in an emergency. A tourniquet is any simple device that can be fashioned around an injured limb to stop bleeding from a severed artery.

Samantha told me that she'd had to apply such a tourniquet to her own arm following a brutal attack several years ago. Samantha shared the following with me:

Samantha was a nineteen-year old college student in 2006. As college students frequently do, she was attending a party with a young man she'd been dating for a while. She told me that there was alcohol at the party, but she herself had never been much of a drinker and was not drinking that night. At some point, Samantha's boyfriend exited the house and walked into the front yard area in front of the residence. She followed only a few seconds behind him. When she walked outside, she saw her boyfriend engaged in an argument with a young lady and approached the two just as the female shoved her boyfriend.

Immediately following her boyfriend getting pushed, Samantha was shoved by the same female offender into the garage. Seconds later, she was flat on her back in the driveway. Two other women in addition to the initial offender jointed the attack, and Samantha was fighting all three just to keep them away from her. The women kicked and punched her. The attack lasted several minutes, but Samantha managed to get free and flee to a safer area, shielded by a friend of hers also in attendance. Upon their retreat, Samantha's friend noticed that she was bleeding heavily from stab wounds.

The punches that Samantha was trying to defend against were actually blows from a broken beer bottle and she'd been stabbed several times. She had stab wounds in her neck and collar bone area as well as others on her arm. Samantha was quickly joined by her boyfriend who gave her his shirt to apply pressure to the wounds. One of the wounds in her arm wouldn't respond to direct pressure, so she asked her boyfriend for his belt which she fashioned into a tourniquet around her arm and above the wound. She continued to tighten it until the bleeding stopped. Samantha was able to seek medical attention later, and I'm happy to say she is well today.

I asked Samantha where she'd learned to secure a tourniquet, but she said she didn't know. She assumed she'd seen it on TV at some point and it stuck with her. Samantha is proof that people can do amazing things when they have no choice. No one was there to help Samantha when she needed it, so the only option was to do it herself. She has since sought out more formalized training in treating such trauma and consulted hawkeyeprepared.com, but at the time of this incident, it was merely a combination of surface knowledge and instinct. She was an individual untrained in life saving measures who applied those measures because she had no other choice.

Samantha's story is indeed incredible and it's important to note that she sought out training after the fact, but the preparation that I'm talking about here occurs in your head. In Samantha's case, she'll never have to convince herself that "This won't happen to me" because it already did. For those who have not yet experienced such trauma, you will have to picture yourself in such a situation. Utilize *When-Then* thinking everywhere you go. *When this happens, then I will do that and if that doesn't work, I will do this.*

This imagery technique can be practiced anywhere. It keeps the mind alert and tuned in to your surroundings. You can practice while driving, shopping, walking down the street, or sitting in a theater or restaurant. You should never think, *when this happens, I will wait for someone else to tell me what to do.* Your life depends on it. Ask yourself: "When this happens, what will work best for me?"

As you change locations throughout the day, what works best for you will change as well, so be sure to reassess and readjust yourself. Know where the exits are in a room and recognize objects in your immediate surroundings that you can use to defend yourself or to make an exit. Don't overlook the obvious, which is sometimes outside the box.

I do presentations and training events on this topic regularly, and when I'm in a venue, I will often ask my audience how many exits they see. They'll usually tell me there's one or two exits to the room because that's how many doors they see. No one even thinks of the wall of windows on the other side of the room. When someone is shooting at you, all bets are off! Break windows, throw chairs, do what is necessary to save your life.

Also remember to keep it simple. As I said before, when someone is shooting at you, you'll be lucky if you can remember your own name. You don't need to frantically wrack your brain for the acronym from some active shooter training video that your employer popped on during your lunch break.

If I asked you what you'd do if your clothes caught on fire, you'd most likely answer with "Stop, Drop, and Roll." We learned it in kindergarten and everybody remembers it. Three little words, because you wouldn't be able to remember much more than that if you were on fire. It has to be simple enough that you can recall it under the most stressful conditions.

It's for that reason that we adhere to the **Run, Hide, Fight** methodology. Engraining those three words in your head will help you categorize your course of action in an active shooter situation. The words don't necessarily go in order, either. Use the mantra as it applies to you. If there's nowhere to run, if there's nowhere to hide, then fight. Fight like your life depends on it, because it does.

I have studied several disciplines of martial arts as well as self-defense systems for work as well as for personal interest. In 1995, I taught a woman's self-defense course with the aid of a certified Rape Prevention Officer. The class taught the use of a weapon called a Yawara stick or Kubotan. About six to seven inches in length, the weapon is gripped in the center of the fist with a small portion of the stick extending on either side of the hand. The ends of the stick are used to strike the attacker in strategic points on the body, and the results can be devastating if you are the recipient. There was also a physical component to the class that allowed the students to practice defending themselves against a simulated attack, enacted by an officer in a padded suit.

Students were initially told to utilize their new skills to ward off the attack to the best of their ability. All were successful. It's important to note that all of the students in this class were women. Most had children or grandchildren. On the second round of simulations, the students were told to defend against the attack as if the attacker was attempting to harm their children or grandchildren. They were told to hold that image in their head as the attack took place.

The difference in response was impressive. The women now not only defended against the original attack, but turned the attacker into the victim. In some cases, we had to separate the student from the officer before the officer was hurt. For the students, defending themselves in real life paled in comparison to defending those they loved. When the class was over, it was clear that any one of the students had the ability to defeat such an attack. The seven inch stick they now possessed was just an aid. The most effective self-defense was based on the use of imagery.

The concept is simple, but the action is tougher. It's always easy to ignore the bad things that happen around you. Stop and smell the roses, but also be aware of the manure. Be alert to your surroundings and practice situational awareness. Be proactive in your preparation and realistic regarding your abilities. Know your limitations.

I once presented to a group of employees at a company sponsored event, and one of the attendees told me that he wasn't concerned about active shooter because his boss was a concealed carry holder. But your boss is not carrying that gun to protect you; he's carrying it to protect himself. There are a lot of liabilities to defense by use of a firearm, and unless you're a law enforcement officer, you had best be protecting your own life.

Yet another presentation attendee tried to argue his lack of concern because he was a black belt in Tae Kwon Do. You can be shot from a great distance; that black belt is useless unless you can actually reach out and touch the bad guy. Additionally, if someone is shooting at you, you won't even remember that you are a black belt.

Your life is a precious, fragile gift. No one cares more about your life than you, so own it. Take responsibility for it and in the case of an active shooter- save it!

9

Opening a Dialogue:

How to discuss active shooter and
lockdown drills with your kids

Parents often ask me when and how they should approach this topic with their kids. I'm no expert in child development, but I am a parent of two wonderful girls who I want to see grow into productive, strong, independent women. As their parent, it is my job to do what I can to ensure they make it there. I recognize that my company does specialize in active shooter response. Coupled with twenty-four years of law enforcement and the fact that my wife is also retired federal law enforcement, it's sometimes the only discussion in our house. We've never sheltered our kids from this topic or any other that would potentially cause them harm if they were unaware.

A shooter doesn't discriminate based on age. How old does your child have to be to become a casualty in an active shooter event? I agree that this is a scary topic and it's unfortunate that we have to prepare our kids for it at all, but it's the world in which we live. You may wonder if you'll be able to explain active shooter preparation in a way that your kids will understand. I would suggest that the first time your kids come home from school and tell you they had a lockdown drill, you start asking questions and open a dialogue with them. Keep in mind that the schools do not always have the best answers either, so find out what they are teaching your kids.

Ask the school questions too, and demand explanations that make sense to you. Be honest with your kids. People will always react in the way that they have been trained and prepared to react, so you must in turn train and prepare your kids. Do not entrust that to someone else. Some schools liken an active shooter to a "mean dog." Tell your kids that they are trying to escape a human being who is killing people, not a "mean dog." If your kids have watched TV or been exposed to the internet, then they've seen violence. It's up to you as the parent to ensure they understand the difference between Hollywood and reality.

My wife and I have discussed this with my kids since they started school, and neither of them suffered negative psychological effects as a result. They haven't been terrified to go to school or suffered sleepless nights. They are, however, better prepared to react to an active shooter situation than any member of the faculty at the schools they've attended. They know how to do what's necessary to save their own lives and because we've discussed it, they won't be herded like sheep if it's not in their best interest.

But what about infants and preschool age kids in a daycare? Preschool kids might not understand this topic, and infants certainly can't take action to save their own lives. I'll reiterate that I'm not an expert in early childhood, but I sought input from Christina Muich, a tenured early childhood professional. The solution in this situation is to make the daycare or facility more difficult to access, train the staff, drill, and review. Muich recommended inquiring with the childcare facility or after-school program regarding their protocol during an active shooter situation. How often do they practice active shooter drills? Any program that can't confidently answer that question is not doing everything in their power to protect the children in their care.

Hawkeye Active Shooter Response once conducted a security assessment on a preschool attached to a community center. The administration acknowledged that there were serious security compromises in the preschool that needed to be addressed. Upon initial review, we were able to enter the facility through multiple unlocked doors. We roamed freely through the halls among students and staff, and no one bothered to ask who we were.

My oldest daughter is a college freshman. During her high school years, I found myself going to the high school many times to deliver forgotten homework or other items. The school has a technology in place that scans your driver's license when you enter the building and runs a basic "instant" background check. (Instant only works for oatmeal). Any background check that returns instant results has very limited value. The problem with this particular technology, or perhaps just this particular system, was that it never scanned my license correctly. It misspelled my last name each and every time. If they had run a background on me, it would've been useless because they had spelled my name wrong. I caught the error and brought it to the attention of the school administration the first time it occurred. The last time I was there, four years after that first incident, it had not been corrected.

This is the technology that the school relied on to detect registered sex offenders and criminals. They lead you to believe that this technology is keeping your kids safe. Don't misunderstand me; they are well-intended and any step in the right direction is progress. But if my child had become a victim because their technology failed to do as intended, then that's just paving the road to hell.

It was not uncommon for this high school (as well as thousands of others) to have an assembly for students and faculty following a high-profile school shooting. I'm not opposed to this type of debriefing, nor am I opposed to a group prayer and a moment of silence. However, an event as horrific as a shooting should also incite improvements to the school's plan of action during such a shooting.

Following one such presentation at my daughter's high school, one of the students approached a faculty member and asked, "If you personally encounter the shooter in the hallway of the school, face to face, what would you do?" The teacher's response was, "I would call 911."

If you're confronted with an active shooter and you stop and reach for your phone to call 911, you are going to be a statistic.

At the beginning of this chapter, I asked the question, "How young is too young?" Let me give you an answer to that.

Think back on your childhood years. At what age do you wish someone had begun to impart this knowledge on you? How many times have you looked back on your life and thought, "I wish I had seen that coming"? How many times did you walk right into something that had a not-so-happy ending, just because you were not aware of your surroundings or not paying attention?

I'm not talking about walking in front of a fast ball while taking the field in a Little League game and taking one in the face (yes, this happened to me.) Times have changed. We're talking about life or death here. Although I will say that if I could turn back time and know what I know now, I would have walked behind the pitcher!

As the parent, you are responsible for teaching your kids. Is there anything more precious or more worth saving? Are you going to entrust this part of their education to technology or the school's approach, or are you going to take control of it? My advice is to talk to your kids as soon as you can and keep talking to them.

10

What I Don't Know Can't Hurt Me:

Unlearning denial and learning to seek
and create opportunities for awareness

Many people have the notion that what they don't know can't hurt them. I don't think I've ever heard anything so ridiculous. What you don't know, or more likely, what you choose to ignore can actually kill you. The reality of active shooter or any other act of senseless violence is not something pleasant to occupy your mind with. I can think of hundreds of other things that I would rather contemplate. But it's because of those pleasant things that we must at least acknowledge the violence, for if we do not, we may no longer be around to daydream about the good things.

Many years ago, I was a gang crimes officer. The community in which I worked suddenly experienced a spike in gang presence. We figured that if we could conquer the problem quickly, we could gain control and maintain control rather than try to play catch-up after the problem had already escalated. One of the ways that we did this was to make contact with as many gang members as possible, especially those being actively recruited into their ranks.

We wanted to identify them, lay the groundwork for a mutual existence, and make certain they understood the rules of mutual existence within our jurisdiction. We would make frequent street stops in order to accomplish this. We gathered names and intelligence, searched cars and even people when we had probable cause or reasonable suspicion to do so. Arrests were made or breaks were given in exchange for better information from new street sources, which led to bigger arrests later on.

I got to know the gang members that frequented the community and they certainly knew me. I eventually began to establish a rapport with some of them. I treated them fairly and in turn, they sought me out when they had details about illegal activity.

No matter how much we got to know each other, it was also important for me to remember that I was not their friend and they were not mine. It was a business deal, one that was never intended to be comfortable and cozy. Most of these gang members were solidly involved in criminal activity and could be dangerous individuals, especially the young recruits trying to gain acceptance from their peers. That being said, having a career in law enforcement is dangerous, and getting the job done requires a certain level of risk.

If I stopped an individual on the street, sometimes I would search him or her, but sometimes I wouldn't. Giving them this occasional pass was likely to result in our receiving information at a later time. I recognize that such a tactic wasn't the safest approach, but it was still a risk that the other officers and I were willing to take.

While on duty one day, I was sitting in an unmarked squad car watching a convenience store across the street. The store was on the east end of town on a main thoroughfare, and was a popular spot for local gang members to stop and steal beer. It was summer, mid-afternoon, and hot. Lounging outside the front of the store was an individual that I'd run into frequently. He was a local gang "hang around," meaning he was trying to make his way up through the ranks of his gang. I watched this individual, who I've given the alias Bobby, from a distance for about ten minutes. He had no idea I was there.

Bobby was unusually nervous, and I had an indication that he was up to no good. Finally, I drove my car into the parking lot of the store and motioned to Bobby to approach the car.

Bobby knew me well and was neither bothered by my presence nor did he hesitate to approach the car. He stood outside the driver's window of my vehicle while I remained in the car, and we struck up a conversation. Tactically, this is the kiss of death. Bobby had the strong upper hand, as I was trapped in the car and he was standing at the window over me. I didn't let my guard down, but I was comfortable with Bobby and chose to take the risk. I'm not too proud of how I handled this situation, and I admit my mistake.

After our conversation, Bobby started to walk away, but I exited the car and said,

"Hold on a second. I can't always let you off that easy. I'm going to pat you down, so put your hands on the hood of my car."

Bobby placed his hands on the car, and I asked him, "Do you have anything on you that you should not have?"

It was hot out. Bobby was only wearing a pair of shorts and a white sleeveless T-shirt. I expected him to simply say, "No sir." Instead he said, "There's a gun in my shorts." My heart sank into my shoes. I told Bobby not to move, requested backup and retrieved the gun from the crotch area of his shorts. I've beat myself up over this case for years. I knew better, and yet I took a stupid unnecessary risk that could've gotten me killed.

If Bobby had wanted to kill me, he was holding all the cards to do so in that moment. Killing a cop would have done wonders for his pursuit of moving up in the gang hierarchy. He would've been a hero in their eyes. I still get angry with myself when I think about the incident. I'm lucky that God was watching me that day because I was not watching myself, and that's the lesson to be learned here. Knowledge is power, and that power exists to protect you. Do not ignore your better judgement. Seek out the knowledge and training you need to prepare yourself for the task at hand and practice it until it becomes instinctual.

Once you've trained those instincts, don't talk yourself out of doing what they tell you. Some challenges in life cannot be reasoned away. In challenges of life and death, there is especially no time for rationalizing. I knew my approach to Bobby was tactically wrong. Sitting in the car with him at my window was a terrible mistake. I'd known it since graduating from the police academy, and yet I did it anyway.

The difference between civilians and law enforcement is that it's the job of law enforcement to look for trouble. It's partially what they're paid to do. Doing so forces them to become trained observers who are less likely to be caught unaware.

As a civilian, you only have to watch out for you. Your job is to train and obtain knowledge for your own benefit, then apply it to stay alive. Do you really want your eulogy to read, "He never saw it coming?" That's little consolation to your friends and family. Your job is to see it coming! You want to anticipate what's around the corner and develop a plan to address it before it happens. I didn't know that Bobby had a gun in his shorts, but I should have anticipated that that could be the case. Ignoring it almost landed me on a slab.

In regards to an active shooter situation, take some time to do research. Find out how different guns function so that if you ever find yourself wrestling over one in order to save your life, you understand how to potentially disable it. If you familiarize yourself with the characteristics of a revolver and a semi-automatic, it could save your life. Understanding the difference between the projectiles of a rifle and those of a shotgun will help you decide what stops the projectile and what hides you from the shooter's view: concealment versus cover.

You don't need to be an armorer to have a basic understanding of guns. I drive a car and if I get a flat tire, I know how to put on the spare, yet I'm not a mechanic. If you take an hour of your spare time and search the internet (as you do for so many other things), you can learn about guns even if you've never seen one in your life.

To say "What you don't know can't hurt you" is the equivalent of an ostrich sticking his head in the sand out of fear. Don't avoid addressing the active shooter threat. I'm telling you that the ostrich is going to get his ass shot off. Whether you're a business owner or just a concerned citizen, you will be the ostrich if you allow yourself to be. You're also just as likely to be the hawk or rattlesnake as you are the ostrich. Saving your own life in these events is your responsibility, and deciding not to be the ostrich is your choice.

11

In God's Time:

God, death, active shooter,
and the decision to survive

I once had a conversation with a close friend about active shooter response, and she told me, "When it's my time, it's just my time," presumably referring to her death at the hands of a shooter. Interestingly enough, this is a comment that I've heard countless times over the years.

No one knows the exact hour that our time on this earth will come to an end. For some, the end comes slowly through a difficult battle with illness, while for others it is abrupt and untimely. Yet I can't wrap my head around the idea of giving up so easily. The thought of throwing your hands in the air and claiming, "Well, I guess it's just my time," and allowing yourself to be extinguished strikes me as extremely selfish.

I have experienced a lot of things in my lifetime and, God willing, I will experience many more. I have become more recently aware of the fact that God has His hand in all things that occur in our lives. My purpose on earth is not mine, but part of a much grander design created by God. This book is not an examination of religious or spiritual beliefs. It's not an analysis of gun control or the root causes of active shooter events. Everyone reading this book has their own beliefs or lack thereof, but when someone is shooting at you, you will probably be calling on God to help! When faced with the prospect of your death, you might pray even if you've never done so before in your life.

Several years ago, I was traveling in the car with my family. I was driving, my wife was in the front passenger seat and my two daughters were in the back. It was mid-afternoon on a weekend, and we were on a family outing.

There was a vehicle in front of us driving at a distance of several car lengths, and my wife, trained to be constantly aware of her surroundings, noticed as it began to swerve erratically. The car continued to move unsteadily, crossing into a lane of oncoming traffic and back again several times. The area of road in question was two lanes, one moving in each direction. An open field occupied the north side of the street. The south side consisted of a banquet hall, and the landscape in front of the building sloped down into a sizable ditch. Just above the ditch, a brick sign displayed the name of the banquet hall.

At this point, the car began to veer off the road on the south side of the street, heading towards the ditch and the wall at an alarming rate. I was able to position my car closer to the vehicle in question and come up on the driver's side of the accelerating car. My wife Carol and I were able to see through the driver's side window, and it was obvious that the driver was dealing with some sort of medical emergency. Carol thought he was having a heart attack and I thought it looked more like a seizure, but in either case he was in big trouble.

The driver, the sole occupant of the car, appeared rigid and trembling. The car was accelerating, meaning he was pressing the gas pedal to the floor. This young man had nearly missed the cars in the other lane numerous times, and we could only hope he wouldn't swerve into traffic again. Eventually, the car accelerated to the point that it moved completely off the road and into the ditch. When it left the ditch, it went airborne. This was no dramatic scene from a spy movie; it merely left the ground slightly, but it did miss that brick wall by only a few feet.

The vehicle came to rest on the curb marking the perimeter of the hall's parking lot. The curb was perfectly centered under the vehicle between the front and rear tires, and the car was pivoting back and forth. That alignment was just enough to keep the rear tires from making contact with the ground. This was fortunate, as the tires were still spinning at speed and the driver continued to seize.

Carol called 911 as we pulled into the parking lot of the banquet hall, and I jumped out of the car to see if I could render aid until EMS and police arrived. I approached the driver's door and opened it, managing to turn the car off and position it in neutral. The driver started to come to, although he was still dazed and confused. I tried to get my adrenaline in check so I could calm him down until help arrived.

The only thing I could think was, "My God, this kid was lucky!" Jesus Himself may as well have been steering that car. As the young man started to come to his senses, I told him he'd had a seizure, been in a car crash, that I was a police officer and that EMS were on the way.

At that moment, I heard a voice. It was a faint woman's voice, calling out the young man's name and saying, "Please talk to me."

Honestly, the first thing that went through my head was, *Oh man! God is talking to me.* The second thing was, *God is a woman! There will be no living in a house full of girls after this revelation.*

As I glanced down between the front seat and driver's side floor board, I saw the driver's cell phone on the floor. The word *Mom* lit up the front screen. I picked up the phone and spoke to the woman on the other end (who was not God, by the way). She was only blocks away and arrived at the scene of the accident to be with her son. I spoke with the young man as he was being loaded into the ambulance, and he told me that the phone had been in his back pocket when he got in the car. He butt dialed his mom when he seized.

As I wished both mother and son well, remaining until the ambulance left, I noticed the one other building on that side of the road: a church. My family and I now attend that church every weekend. I also serve on their security team.

I said before that I have a tremendous faith in God and all that He does in our lives. Even if I did not, I must say that the events of that day would've changed my mind. I have seen plenty of instances of God's intervention, but never anything else quite like that. I never heard from that family again, but I trust it all turned out well.

Sometimes God's intervention is not limited to parting the Red Sea. He gives each and every one of us special abilities and knowledge. There is something I can learn from everyone I meet, and conversely I can teach something to everyone, too. Every person plays a role in a larger picture, and there's not a single life that is without purpose.

The world is not evil, but there is evil in the world. If you're stuck in an active shooter situation, that's you being confronted with evil and I'm going to argue that God wants you to fight it. If you cannot find the strength to fight for yourself, fight for those that count on you, some of whom you might not have met yet.

I have a wonderful wife and two fantastic daughters. We count on each other every single day. I can't imagine not having any one of them in my world. My daughters count on me to be at their graduations and to walk them down the aisle on their wedding day. Perhaps the grandchildren that I haven't met yet are counting on me, too. The ability to be there for them is a God-given gift, and I will not allow evil to take it away. If God has determined that it is "just my time," He can take me with a heart attack, any number of ailments, or just vaporize me for that matter. He doesn't have to send someone through the door armed with a gun to end your life.

If you were diagnosed with cancer tomorrow, wouldn't you seek treatment? Will you sit down with your family and tell them that if you ever become sick, you're going to accept it as "your time" and call it quits? How about if someone you cared about chose to give in so easily; would you accept it?

This is not any different. If you become sick, God provides you with modern medicine to enhance His grace. If you're stuck in a room with an active shooter, He provides you with the strength to save yourself!

Adhering to this mindset doesn't mean that fighting as a last resort is guaranteed to save your life. But if you don't try, you will certainly be just another statistic and those that are counting on you will be left without you.

I can't make this decision for you. I can't formulate a plan for you. You have to do those things for yourself.

Not so long ago, during a class that I was taking, someone asked me, "Why do you do what you do?" Here's my answer. Hawkeye Active Shooter Response does what we do so that people will save themselves, so that businesses will protect themselves and their employees. I do this so that people will understand that no one is going to get there in time to save them. I do this because I know these methods work, but only if you take responsibility for yourself. I've grown exhausted of seeing press releases in the aftermath of active shooter events where witnesses are quoted as saying, "I never thought this could happen here."

Why do I do this? I want to train and enlighten people so that instead, I can start to see survivors on television saying, "We trained for this. As a result, I'm still alive. I guess it just wasn't my time." I want those survivors to be able to walk off camera and go home to the people who count on them. As Lt. Col Jeff Cooper once said, **"If violent crime is to be curbed, it is only the intended victim who can do it. The felon does not fear the police, and he fears neither judge nor jury. Therefore what he must be taught to fear is his victim."**[1]

---

[1] Cooper, Jeff. *Principles of Personal Defense*. Boulder, CO: Paladin Press, 2006.

Acknowledgements

There are a number of people that I would like to thank for their influence and input into this book. This wouldn't have been possible without any of them.

Thank you to my wonderful wife Carol, my harshest critic and yet my biggest motivator, for all her support.

Thank you to my daughters, Peyton and Makenna, whose encouragement and undying interest in my stories and pursuit of reality were the catalyst for this undertaking. A special thanks to Peyton for putting her talents to work as the editor of this book.

To my partners at Hawkeye Active Shooter Response: Carol Skoczylas, Joe Jungles and Ray Garza, thanks for believing in our mission and sharing my vision.

Thank you to Samantha and SH for your contributions to this book. I'm grateful that you're both alive today to tell your stories.

Thank you to Christina Muich for adding insight into the inner workings of early childhood learning and retention.

To the Hawkeye Instructors: your skills and experience are truly helping to save lives.

To my co-presenters Kyle Cochran of Vista Safety Consulting and Amber Cox of Laner Muchin: your insight and expertise help cover all the bases of liability and exposure and create dynamic presentations.

Finally, and most importantly, thanks to God for allowing me to have the experiences that I've had and for giving me the ability to impart my knowledge in order to save lives.

About the Author

Dan Skoczylas grew up in the southwest suburbs of Chicago, Illinois. He graduated from Victor J. Andrew High School in Tinley Park and became interested in law enforcement after participating in a police cadet program in Oak Lawn where his father had served as a police officer for thirteen years. After graduating high school, Dan pursued criminal justice classes at a community college while simultaneously testing for local police departments.

Dan was hired by the Hickory Hills Police Department at the age of twenty-one and graduated from the Police Training Institute (PTI) in 1989. He first served as a patrolman for the Hickory Hills Police Department from 1989-1995 before developing the department's Tactical-Gang Crimes Unit, where he served from 1993-1995.

In 1997, Dan was assigned to the US Customs Task Force in Chicago and joined a money laundering/narcotics smuggling investigations team. He remained there until 1999.

Dan returned to the Hickory Hills Police Department in 1999 as a Detective and member of the department's High Risk Entry Team. After being promoted to Sergeant in 2001, he attended the Southern Police Institute School of Command Development. He was promoted to Lieutenant in 2007.

In 2014, Dan retired from the Hickory Hills Police Department. Dan is a founding principal of CLS Background Investigations (2001), Makton Investigations (2006), and Hawkeye Active Shooter Response Training (2014). Today, he educates civilians throughout the US on background investigations and active shooter response.

Dan currently lives in Illinois with his wife Carol and two daughters, Peyton and Makenna.

Made in the USA
Columbia, SC
03 March 2020